First Facts®

Staying Safe

Staying Safe around Strangers

by Lucia Raatma

CAPSTONE PRESS
a capstone imprint

First Facts is published by Capstone Press,
1710 Roe Crest Drive, North Mankato, Minnesota 56003.
www.capstonepub.com

 Books published by Capstone Press are manufactured with paper
containing at least 10 percent post-consumer waste.

Library of Congress Cataloging-in-Publication Data
Raatma, Lucia.
 Staying safe around strangers / by Lucia Raatma.
     p. cm.—(First facts. Staying safe)
 Includes bibliographical references and index.
 Summary: "Discusses rules and techniques for staying safe around strangers"—Provided by
publisher.
 ISBN 978-1-4296-6821-7 (library binding)
 ISBN 978-1-4296-7195-8 (paperback)
 1. Children and strangers—Juvenile literature. 2. Safety education—Juvenile literature. 3. Crime
prevention—Juvenile literature. 4. Kidnapping—Prevention—Juvenile literature. I. Title.
 HQ784.S8R33 2012
 613.6083—dc22   2011009999

Editorial Credits

Rebecca Glaser and Christine Peterson, editors; Ted Williams, designer;
    Svetlana Zhurkin, media researcher; Laura Manthe, production specialist

Photo Credits

All photos by Capstone Studio/Karon Dubke except:
Getty Images/Nivek Neslo, 15

Essential content terms are **bold** and are defined at the bottom of the spread where they first appear.

Printed in the United States of America in North Mankato, Minnesota.
122011   006506R

Table of Contents

Who Are Strangers?

You see new people every day. Some people look friendly. Others seem scary. But they all have one thing in common. They are strangers.

Strangers are people you have never met. Most people are nice. But some people are not. By following a few rules, you can be safe around strangers.

Trusted Adults

How can you tell which adults to trust? **Trusted adults** are people such as your parents, teachers, and **counselors**. Police officers and firefighters are also adults you can trust. Ask your parents what other adults can help you stay safe.

trusted adult—**a grown-up you know who is honest and reliable** counselor—**someone trained to help with problems or give advice**

Know the Difference

Some strangers aren't nice. They may want to hurt people. They sometimes use tricks to get closer to kids. They may offer you candy, money, or a ride home.

Some people may trick kids by asking for help. They might ask you to help find a lost pet or for directions. But don't be fooled. These adults don't really need your help. Adults should never ask children for help.

No Thanks

To stay safe, never take anything from people you don't know. Don't talk to strangers or answer any questions without a parent's permission.

Never go anywhere with people you do not know. Don't get into a stranger's car or enter their home. Say no and run away if strangers ask you to go somewhere.

permission—the OK to do something

Power in Numbers

One way to stay safe is to stick together in groups. Some people look for children who are alone. Stay safe by going places with others. Make sure you have a trusted adult along too. If you get lost, find a police officer or other trusted adult for help.

Safe Way Home

When walking with friends, be sure to follow a safe route. With a trusted adult, find the best way to walk to and from school. It's safest to walk where there are other people. Make sure your route has good sidewalks and lights.

route—the regular path you follow to go somewhere

Keep Your Distance

You pass different people all the time. Always keep a safe distance between you and others. Try to stay three arm lengths away from other people.

If someone makes you feel unsafe, take a step back. Then turn around and run away in the opposite direction.

opposite—facing or moving the other way

17

Yell No and Go

If a stranger approaches you, use your voice. Yell for help loudly. Tell people the person isn't your parent. If you are grabbed, fall to the ground. Kick to get free of the person's hold.

Once you break free, run away quickly. Go to a public place such as a library or store. Have a trusted adult call 9-1-1.

You Have the Power

You have the power to stay safe. Stay close to a parent or trusted adult. Don't talk to or go with people you don't know. Yell loudly, run away, and get help.

Hands On:
Code Words

Learn to be smarter than strangers by choosing a family code word. Code words can help you tell a trusted adult from a stranger. Gather your family to choose a code word. Then practice using the word.

What You Do

1. Choose a word that everyone can remember. The word should be hard for others to guess. Avoid using your pets' names or names of popular TV or movie characters.
2. Make sure everyone in your family knows the code word. Do not tell anyone else your code word.
3. Practice using your code word with your family. Your parents should pretend they are someone else picking you up. If they say the code word, you know it's safe to go with them.
4. Your parents should use the code word in an emergency. They might send an adult they trust to pick you up. They will tell that person the code word. That person should tell you the code word.
5. Never go with anyone who does not know your code word.

Glossary

counselor (KOUN-suh-lur)—someone trained to help with problems or give advice

opposite (OP-uh-zit)—facing or moving the other way

permission (pur-MISH-uhn)—the OK to do something

route (ROUT)—the regular path you follow to go somewhere

trusted adult (TRUHS-tud uh-DUHLT)—a grown-up you know who is honest and reliable

Read More

Barraclough, Sue. *Your Own Safety.* Stay Safe. Chicago: Heinemann Library, 2008.

Donahue, Jill Urban. *Say No and Go: Stranger Safety.* How to Be Safe! Minneapolis: Picture Window Books, 2009.

Johnson, Jinny. *Being Safe.* Now We Know About. New York: Crabtree Pub. Company, 2010.

Internet Sites

FactHound offers a safe, fun way to find Internet sites related to this book. All of the sites on FactHound have been researched by our staff.

Here's all you do:

Visit *www.facthound.com*

Type in this code: 9781429668217

Check out projects, games and lots more at
www.capstonekids.com

Index